MITZIE WILSON

ICE CREAMS & COLD DESSERTS

HAMLYN

NOTE

1. Metric and imperial measurements have been calculated separately. Use one set of measurements only as they are not exact equivalents.
2. All spoon measures are level unless otherwise stated.

We would like to thank:
Wedgewood China and the Covent Garden General Store, Covent Garden WC2 for the loan of china and glass; Celine Hampsey and Denise Clark for typing the manuscript, Lorrie Mack and Gilly Cubitt for loan of props; Nichola Palmer and Jackie Lambert for help with recipe tasting; Home Economics students from Croydon College, Carol Greaves, Karen Gough, Sue Inglesia, Penny Baker and Amanda Fries for their assistance during photography, and
Donald Brown for
his help and support.

Produced by New Leaf Productions
Photography by Mick Duff
Design by Jim Wire
Series Editor: Elizabeth Gibson
Typeset by System Graphics

First published in 1985 by
Hamlyn Publishing
Bridge House, 69 London Road
Twickenham, Middlesex, England

ISBN 0 600 32498 2

Printed in Spain

Larsa D. L. TF. 554 – 1985

CONTENTS

HOW TO USE GELATINE

Many cold sweets are set with gelatine. Don't be afraid to use it; once you know how, it's simple! Use the quantities stated in the individual recipe.

Place cold liquid in a small bowl. Sprinkle the gelatine over (never the other way around). Stand bowl in a small saucepan with hot water 2.5cm/1in up the side of the bowl. Place pan over a low heat and stir until the gelatine dissolves and the liquid is clear.

To add to desserts, pour the gelatine in a thin stream onto the mixture, beating continuously so that the gelatine is quickly and evenly dispersed.

Try to have the mixture at room temperature before you add the gelatine. If it is too chilled, the gelatine may set into thin ropes; if this happens, strain the mixture and add more gelatine.

15g/½oz/3 teaspoons gelatine will set 500ml/1 pint of mixture.

FAVOURITE ICE CREAM RECIPES

All you need to know about making home-made ice cream

HOME-MADE ICE CREAM

Home-made ice cream: there's nothing quite like it. Yet it needn't be regarded as a luxury or just for the kids. It's so simple to make, and the variety of flavours is endless. Once the ice-cream is in the freezer, you've got instant desserts at hand for almost every day of the week. Just follow one of the basic recipes and add fruit, nuts, crushed biscuits, or even chopped sweets.

Ice cream is based on custard made from egg yolks, sugar and cream. Obviously the more cream and eggs, the richer the dessert. The custard base can also be made from half milk half cream, or made from custard powder with cream, evaporated milk or even dessert topping.

Ingredients

The amount of sugar in the recipe is vital to both ice cream and sorbets; it's not just to sweeten the dessert. Too much sugar and the ice cream will not freeze; not enough sugar and the ice will be too hard to scoop. It is wise to follow the amount in the recipe, although you can experiment by reducing the sugar slightly if desired. Unrefined sugars can also be used but will give a definite toffee-treacle flavour to all recipes. Honey can also be used. Remember that the sweetness weakens in taste when the ice cream is frozen.

Alcohol also stops ice cream and sorbets from freezing. Ice creams with a little alcohol will be soft to scoop, but too much alcohol and the recipe will never freeze hard.

Equipment

Ice creams and sorbets should have a smooth, creamy consistency, and the only way to achieve this is by breaking up the ice crystals that form. It is not necessary to use ice cream makers—an ordinary deep freeze or freezer compartment of the fridge will produce excellent results—but you do have to stir the ice frequently during freezing to get a smooth, creamy consistency.

Ice Cream Churns: These will do the hard work for you but are expensive. The traditional ice cream churn is a wooden bucket with a metal container inside fitted with manually operated paddles. The bucket is packed with ice and salt, and the ice cream is churned inside the metal container. Although this produces a superb result, few of us have a continuous supply of ice, and it is very time-consuming.

Electric ice cream churn: Based on the traditional churn, this one takes the hard work out of ice cream making, electrically operating the paddles until the ice cream is too stiff to churn; but do remember you still need a continuous supply of ice.

Food Processors: These are a great help in turning the fruit to a fine purée in only a few seconds. Some models now also include freezer trays for ice cream and sorbet recipes. When the ice is frozen it fits neatly down the feeder tube into the processor bowl. A special plastic blade then gently stirs the ice to a fine, smooth mixture—perfect for immediate serving.

Fully Automatic Ice Cream and Sorbet Maker: The most convenient—but also the most expensive—ice cream maker, it electrically churns and freezes at the same time and takes only 20 minutes to produce perfect results. It can make from .5–1.5 litres/1–3 pints, is simple, automatic and easy to clean. A worthwhile investment if you intend to make a lot of ice cream, it is nevertheless a large appliance, so you need plenty of work or storage space.

Electric Ice Cream Maker: Simply two metal containers with an electric motor that fits in the middle and operates two paddles to stir the mixture. The machine operates in the freezer, so you will need an electric point nearby and a flat surface in the freezer.

To freeze ice cream and sorbets
Freeze ice cream and sorbets as quickly as possible for the best texture. If making ice cream or sorbets in the freezer compartment of the refrigerator, remember to set it to its coldest temperature at least an hour beforehand. If using a freezer, turn it to 'Quick' or 'Fast' freeze.

Use shallow metal containers for freezing ice cream and sorbets so that the mixture will freeze faster; but for acidic fruits use only stainless steel.

Make sure you clear a flat level surface in the freezer, preferably on the bottom or against the sides of the freezer, so that the mixture comes in contact with a really cold surface and thus freezes quickly.

To store
Transfer the ice cream or sorbet to a plastic container, cover with a lid, and label. Try to store in the right sized containers. If the ice cream is only half full, or only half is eaten at one meal, cover the mixture with freezer film so that ice crystals don't form on the mixture and ruin the texture. Ice cream will store for up to 3 months. After that it begins to shrink, and over a very long period of time the fat may turn rancid.

Never refreeze melted ice cream. If it has merely softened a little it can be refrozen, but the texture may have deteriorated.

To serve
Ice cream ripens after it has been made, so always try to leave it frozen a couple of hours before serving.

Most home-made ice creams, except those made with alcohol, are too hard to scoop straight from the freezer, so they should be allowed to soften before serving. Leave the ice cream in the refrigerator for about 30 minutes; never at room temperature unless in an emergency, or you'll find the outside will melt and the inside still be hard. Scoop ice cream using a tablespoon or ice cream scoopers, or for tiny balls of ice cream use a melon baller.

To unmold ice cream and sorbet desserts, dip mould in warm water for a few seconds just to melt the inside slightly. Invert onto a plate and lift off the mould. Then leave dessert to soften in the refrigerator.

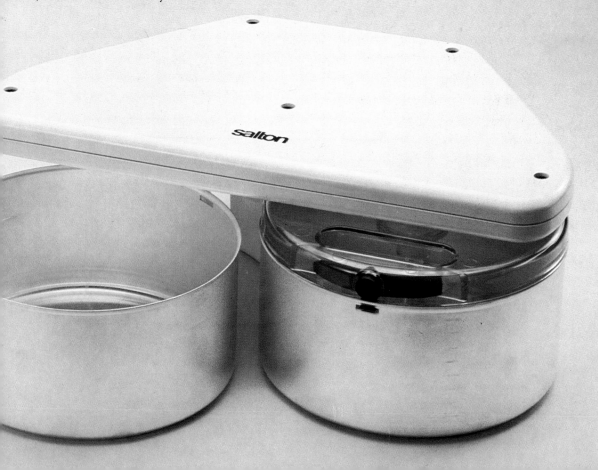

FRUIT ICES

Fruit ices—whether sorbets, water ices or ice creams—are the perfect way to capture the flavour of seasonal fruits for the whole year. Use fruits when they are at their natural best, which is often when they are cheaper, too. Frozen and drained, canned fruits, and fruit juices can all be used to make excellent ices.

Firm fruit such as apples, pears, plums, apricots and cherries need cooking to soften the fruit. Poach them in sugar syrup (see recipe p.20) until tender; then push through a sieve to remove skin and stones.

Soft fruit such as strawberries, raspberries, red- and blackcurrants, melons, blackberries, peaches, mangos, kiwi fruit and pineapple can simply be puréed either by pushing the fruit—peeled if necessary—through a sieve or blending it in a liquidiser (strain to remove pips if desired.) Then for every 300ml/½ pint puree add 100g/4oz sugar.

Dried fruits such as apricots, prunes, dates, figs, apples and pears should be soaked overnight in cold water, simmered until tender and then puréed. Then for every 300ml/½ pint of purée add 100g/4oz sugar.

Unsweetened fruit juices such as orange, grapefruit, pineapple, apple and exotic fruit juice blends can also be used. Simply dissolve 100g/4oz sugar in 300ml/½ pint of fruit juice and cool. This quantity of sugar is needed to help freeze the dessert. If using freshly squeezed juice, add the grated rind too.

ECONOMICAL ICE CREAM
Serves 6

300ml/½ pint custard (made from 1 tablespoon custard powder, or use canned or instant custard)
1 teaspoon vanilla flavouring
150ml/¼ pint double cream OR
1 170-g/6-oz can evaporated milk OR
1 packet dessert topping

Allow custard to cool. Stir in vanilla flavouring. Whip cream, evaporated milk or dessert topping until thick, and fold into custard. Pour into a container and freeze for 1 hour or until frozen 2.5cm/1in in from sides. Scrape into a chilled bowl and beat mixture until smooth. Refreeze until firm.

Chocolate: Stir 50g/2oz plain chocolate into custard before cooling.

Coffee: Omit vanilla and add 1 tablespoon instant coffee, dissolved in 1 tablespoon hot water.

VARIATIONS

Liquorice Ice Cream: A ghastly-looking, gorgeous-tasting ice cream the kids will love. Surprisingly popular with grown ups too! Omit vanilla flavouring and melt 100g/4oz liquorice toffees in the milk before making the custard.

Choc-Chip Ice Cream: Simply stir 4 crushed chocolate flake bars into ice cream halfway through freezing.

Raspberry Ripple Ice Cream: Stir 4 tablespoons raspberry jam into the ice cream halfway through freezing.

Marshmallow Ice Cream: Another favourite with children, this ice cream has "chewy bits" in it! Omit the vanilla flavouring and melt half of a 200-g/7.5-oz packet of marshmallows in the milk before making the custard. Halfway through the freezing, stir in the remaining marshmallows, snipped into quarters (use wet scissors).

CUSTARD AND CREAM ICE CREAM

Makes .5 litre/1 pint
Serves 6

Made from a real egg custard, this is the traditional ice cream recipe.

1 egg
1 egg yolk
3 tablespoons caster sugar
300ml/½ pint milk
1 vanilla pod or 2–3 drops vanilla flavouring
150ml/¼ pint double cream

Lightly beat whole egg, yolk and sugar together. Heat the milk (with the vanilla pod if used) to just below boiling point. Pour onto the egg mixture beating continuously. Return to the pan and stir over a low heat until the mixture is the consistency of single cream. Do not overcook or the egg will curdle; if this happens blend mixture in a liquidiser. Allow to cool completely. Remove vanilla pod. Whip the cream until it just holds its shape. Fold into the custard. Pour into a container and freeze for 1 hour or until frozen 2.5cm/1in in from sides. Scrape into a chilled bowl and beat mixture until smooth. Refreeze until firm.

VARIATIONS

Pistachio Ice Cream
Roughly chop 50g/2oz unsalted pistachio nuts and add to the milk before heating. Omit vanilla and add pistachio or almond flavouring instead.

Spiced Honey
Follow the basic recipe adding 3 tablespoons runny honey instead of sugar. Add ½ teaspoon ground cinnamon and a pinch of ground cloves.

Pina Colada
Omit vanilla flavouring from basic recipe. Dissolve 100g/4oz creamed coconut in the milk. Liquidise

until smooth. Fold in 2 tablespoons coconut liqueur with the cream. Serve with pineapple pieces.

Brandy Cream
Omit vanilla flavouring from basic recipe. Make egg custard with just 150ml/¼ pint milk. Allow to cool then stir in 150ml/¼ pint Brandy Cream Liqueur and the whipped cream. Serve in Chocolate Trellis Cups (see p.62).

Rich Chocolate
Omit vanilla from the basic recipe and melt 100g/4oz plain dark chocolate in the milk. Decorate with Chocolate shapes (see p.62).

RICH VANILLA ICE CREAM
Makes .5 litre/1 pint. Serves 6

Made by the syrup and egg yolk method, this makes a light, soft ice cream that needs only a short time in the refrigerator to soften for serving.

50g/2oz caster sugar
3 egg yolks
300ml/½ pint double cream
1 teaspoon vanilla flavouring

Place sugar and 4 tablespoons water in a small saucepan. Heat slowly until sugar has dissolved. Bring to the boil and boil for 3 minutes. Dip two teaspoons into syrup, cool for a few moments, then press spoons back to back, pull apart. If a sticky thread forms between the spoons, the syrup is ready. If not, boil for a little longer, or until syrup reaches 220°F/108°C on a sugar thermometer. Place egg yolks in a bowl. Whisk sugar syrup onto egg yolks until thick and foamy. Whip cream until it just holds its shape and fold into egg mixture with the vanilla. Pour into a container, cover and freeze for 1 hour or until frozen 2.5cm/1in in from sides. Scrape into a chilled bowl and whisk mixture smooth. Refreeze until firm.

VARIATIONS

Banana and Sunflower
Make up basic recipe using muscovado sugar instead of caster sugar. Omit vanilla. Mash 4 very ripe bananas with 2 tablespoons lemon juice. Fold into the egg yolk mixture with the cream. Serve scattered with sunflower seeds, and a banana "flower".

Apple and Prune
Omit the vanilla flavouring, but make up the basic recipe. Cook 500g/1lb peeled, cored and sliced cooking apples with 50g/2oz sugar. Drain 1 440-g/15½-oz can of prunes. Stone the fruit and add to the apple with ½ teaspoon cinnamon. Blend together in a liquidiser and fold into ice cream with the cream.

Strawberry and Cointreau
Omit the vanilla flavouring, but make up basic recipe. Mash 500g/1lb strawberries to a pulp. Stir into ice cream mixture with 3 tablespoons Cointreau. Serve in Biscuit baskets, (recipe p.63).

Apricot and Almond
Omit vanilla flavouring but make up basic recipe. Poach 500g/1lb fresh stoned apricots in 4 tablespoons sweet white wine (or sugar syrup). Mash to a pulp and stir into ice cream with 50g/2oz ground almonds and ½ teaspoon almond flavouring. Freeze in a 1 litre/2 pint mould if liked.

MERINGUE ICE

Serves 6

A soft, speedy ice cream that doesn't need beating and scoops straight from the fridge.

4 eggs, separated
100g/4oz caster sugar
300ml/½ pint double cream

Beat the egg yolks in a small bowl until blended. In a larger, clean, greasefree bowl whisk the egg whites until stiff but not dry. Add the sugar 1 tablespoon at a time whisking continuously until the mixture is stiff and glossy. Whip the cream until it forms soft peaks. Using a metal spoon, carefully fold the yolks, whites and cream together. Pour into a container and freeze until firm.

VARIATIONS

Christmas Candied Bombe:

Soak 175g/6oz mixture of dried apricots, glacé pineapple, cocktail or glacé cherries, or raisins in 6 tablespoons rum or brandy. Cover and leave overnight. Stir into the mixture and pour into a pudding basin lined with a double layer of cling film. Freeze until firm. Gather up cling film and twist into a ball. Roll ice into a neat round shape and freeze again. Serve with whipped cream or melted chocolate poured over.

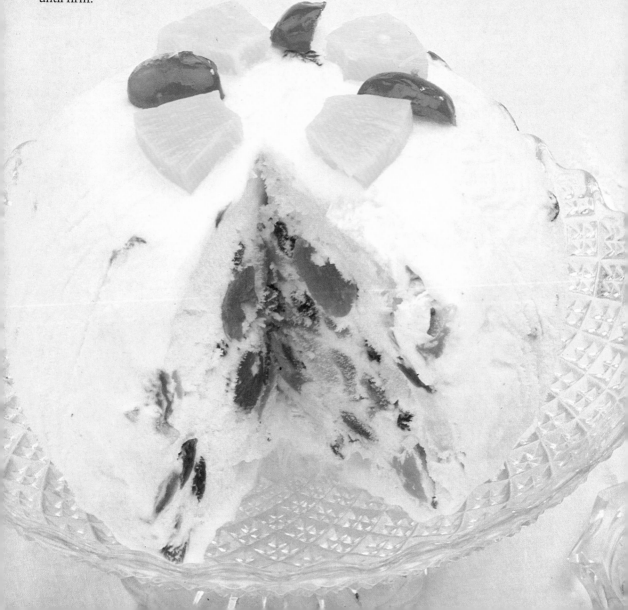

Cherry and Kirsch

Stir 3 tablespoons of Kirsch or cherry brandy into ice cream. Drain the juice from 1 396-g/14-oz can of black or red cherries into a saucepan. Stir in 2 teaspoons cornflour and bring to the boil; stirring cook for 1 minute. Add cherries and cool. Stir into meringue ice cream mixture and freeze. Serve topped with maraschino cherries.

Autumn Ice

Purée 225g/8oz blackberries and cook 1 large peeled cooking apple to a purée. Cool. Stir apple and blackberry purée into ice cream mixture before freezing. Alternatively, use a can of pie filling. Serve with Blackberry coulis (recipe p.26).

Toffee Crisp

Heat 50g/2oz butter with 2 tablespoons golden syrup and 2 tablespoons muscovado sugar in a small pan until butter melts. Cook for 1 minute. Stir in 50g/2oz Rice Krispie breakfast cereal. Cool, then stir into meringue ice cream. Serve with extra cereal.

UNUSUAL ICES

HAZELNUT CHEESE ICE CREAM
Serves 4–6

50g/2oz hazelnuts
225g/7oz full fat soft cheese
40g/1½oz caster sugar
150ml/¼ pint milk
2 tablespoons double cream
few drops vanilla essence

Toast hazelnuts under a hot grill until skins split. Rub hazelnuts in a tea towel to remove skins. Finely chop nuts. Cream the cheese and sugar together until smooth, gradually whisk in the milk, cream and vanilla essence. Stir in the hazelnuts. Pour into a container, cover and freeze for 1 hour or until partially frozen. Scrape into a chilled bowl, and whisk until smooth. Refreeze until firm.

YOGURT ICE
For 4–6 portions

Creamy yet with a refreshing tang, this ice cream is made in minutes and is lighter on calories and cost. Use any sweetened fruit flavoured yogurt, but for natural yogurt increase the sugar by 50g/2oz.

2 teaspoons gelatine
50g/2oz caster sugar
170-g/6-oz can evaporated milk, chilled
300ml/12oz fruit-flavoured yogurt

Dissolve gelatine in 3 tablespoons water (see p.3); stir in sugar. Beat evaporated milk until thick; gradually whisk in the gelatine mixture, then the yogurt. Pour into a container, cover and freeze until frozen 2.5cm/1in in from sides. Turn into a bowl, whisk until smooth. Refreeze 1 hour or until firm.

If desired, chop additional fresh, drained or canned fruit, and serve with the ice.

BROWN BREAD ICE CREAM

Toasted breadcrumbs give this ice cream a chewy, nutty texture. Use brown sugar in the basic ice cream and to sweeten the breadcrumbs too.

For 1 quantity Economical vanilla ice cream or Rich vanilla ice cream:

50g/2oz brown breadcrumbs
50g/2oz soft brown or caster sugar

Set oven at 200°C/400°F/Gas 6. Place breadcrumbs on a baking tray and sprinkle with sugar. Bake for 10 minutes until golden brown. Cool until they become crunchy. Break up and stir crumbs into partially frozen ice cream. Refreeze until firm.

KULFI
Serves 4

An Indian dessert that is made from reduced milk, deliciously flavoured with cardamon pods. Just add sugar to taste. It takes about 1 hour of careful simmering, so cook this milk when you're busy doing other things in the kitchen.

1.15 litre/2 pints milk
5 whole white cardamon pods
2 tablespoons sugar
2 tablespoons chopped almonds
25g/1oz unsalted pistachio nuts

Place the milk in a heavy-based saucepan (preferably non-stick). Heat to just below boiling point. Add cardamon pods and lower the heat so that the milk quietly simmers for about 1 hour, or until the milk is reduced to about a third of its original volume: about 450ml/¾ pint. Stir frequently to break up the skin. Remove cardamon pods, add sugar, almonds and half the pistachios. Pour into a freezer container and allow to cool. Freeze for 30 minutes; take out every 30 minutes or so and beat with a fork to break up crystals. When it is frozen but still soft enough to scoop, divide it between individual moulds or yogurt pots. Freeze firm, then turn out and top with remaining pistachios.

SORBETS, WATER ICES AND GRANITAS

SORBETS

A true sorbet is based on a lemon- or orange-flavoured syrup with extra fruit juice or purée added. Gelatine is added to soften the consistency, and whisked egg white is folded in half way through the freezing to give a light, fluffy consistency. A sherbet usually refers to a sorbet to which whipped cream is added.

LEMON SORBET
Makes 900ml/1½ pints

600ml/1 pint water
225g/8oz granulated sugar
rind of 2 lemons
300ml/½ pint lemon juice
3 teaspoons gelatine
2 egg whites

Place water and sugar together in a small pan. Heat gently until sugar dissolves. Bring to the boil, and boil steadily for 10 minutes. Cool. Dissolve gelatine in 3 tablespoons of water (see p.3) and whisk into syrup with the lemon rind and juice. Pour into a container, cover and freeze for about 1 hour, until partially frozen. Scrape into a chilled bowl and beat lightly to break up crystals. Whisk egg white until stiff but not dry and carefully fold into ice mixture. Refreeze for a further 1½ hours; whip again and freeze until firm.

VARIATIONS:

Orange Wallbangers
Make as for lemon sorbet using orange juice and adding 3 tablespoons Galliano liqueur before freezing. Freeze in scooped-out orange shells.

Grapefruit and Crème de Menthe
Make as for lemon sorbet, using grapefruit juice and adding 3 tablespoons Crème de Menthe liqueur before freezing. Serve with Crème de Menthe poured over.

Dry Martini on the Rocks
Make as for lemon sorbet adding 4 tablespoons dry vermouth. Decorate with lemon and cucumber slices.

Iced Passionate Kiss
Scoop seed and juice out of 4 passion fruits (or use 4 tablespoons bottled passion fruit juice) and mix with 200ml/7oz orange juice. Make as for lemon sorbet. Serve with a little extra passion fruit.

KIWI AND COINTREAU CUPS
Serves 4

Choose fairly firm fruit for this recipe, or the fruit shells will collapse.

4 large kiwi fruit
2 tablespoons Cointreau
100g/4oz caster sugar
1 egg white
150ml/¼ pint whipping cream

Cut the top off of each kiwi fruit, and with a teaspoon carefully scoop out the flesh leaving a little around the skin to make a firm container. Purée the fruit in a liquidiser or mash finely. Stir in Cointreau and sugar. Freeze the kiwi cups and the sorbet until firm. Turn sorbet into a bowl, beat until smooth. Whisk egg white until stiff but not dry, and whip cream until it just holds its shape. Fold egg whites and cream into fruit mixture. Spoon into kiwi cups (or in a freezer container). Top with the fruit "lids." Pack the fruits tightly together in a container so that they will stand upright and freeze until firm.
Place in refrigerator 20 minutes before serving.

FRUIT SORBET
Makes 1 litre/2 pints

600ml/1 pint water
225g/8oz granulated sugar
600ml/1 pint fruit purée ie. raspberry,
strawberry, blackcurrant, gooseberry,
melon, apricot made from about 1kg/2lb
fruit
2 egg whites, whisked

Prepare sugar and water syrup as for lemon sorbet. Cool. Add the fruit purée to the syrup and freeze as before. Fold in egg whites and refreeze. Gelatine is not added to fruit sorbets, which are generally softer, because of the additional fruit and egg white.

APPLE SORBET

Use any bottled fruit-flavoured syrup in the same way.

1 tablespoon gelatine
450ml/¾ pint apple-flavoured syrup
3 egg whites

Dissolve gelatine in 2 tablespoons water (see p.3). Beat into the apple syrup with 450ml/¾ pint water. Pour into a freezer tray and freeze until mushy. Turn into a bowl and beat until smooth. Whisk egg whites until stiff but not dry. Fold into ice and refreeze until firm.

POMEGRANATE ROSE SORBET
Makes ½ litre/1 pint
Serves 6–8

This sorbet is delicately rose-scented and refreshing.

350g/12oz sugar
1 tablespoon gelatine
2 pomegranates
2 teaspoons rose-water
1 egg white

Place sugar and 450ml/¾ pint water in a saucepan. Heat gently until sugar dissolves, bring to the boil, and boil for 10 minutes. Cool. Dissolve gelatine in 3 tablespoons water (see p.3). Stir into sugar syrup. Roll 1 pomegranate firmly on a hard surface to loosen seeds. Halve pomegranate. Place seeds in a sieve and press with a wooden spoon to extract as much juice as possible. Stir the juice into syrup with the rose-water Pour into a container and freeze for 1 hour or until partially frozen. Scrape into a chilled bowl, and beat lightly. Whisk egg white until stiff but not dry, fold into sorbet and refreeze until firm.

WATER ICES

Water ices are simply fruit purées added to sugar syrup with a little gelatine to soften the consistency.

BASIC RECIPE

Serves 4

1 teaspoon gelatine
150ml/¼ pint sugar syrup (recipe below)
300ml/½ pint fruit purée

Dissolve the gelatine in the sugar syrup. Stir the fruit purée into the syrup. Pour into a shallow container; cover and freeze. Whisk mixture frequently to break up the ice crystals during freezing.

SUGAR SYRUP

100g/4oz sugar or honey
rind and juice of 1 lemon
300ml/½ pint water

Place sugar or honey, lemon rind, juice and water in a small pan. Heat gently until sugar has dissolved. Bring to the boil and boil for 5 minutes. Cool.

WATER ICE VARIATIONS

Melon & Ginger: Cut 1 small melon in half (using a zigzag action to vandyke them). Discard seeds and scoop out the flesh to make 300ml/½ pint of purée. Stir this into sugar syrup and gelatine with 4 pieces stem ginger chopped and 2 tablespoons of the ginger syrup. Freeze as basic recipe. Freeze melon shells; then when the water ice is a slushy consistency, pour into the shells to freeze again. Thaw for 20 minutes in fridge before serving. Alternatively serve one type of melon water ice in a contrasting melon cup.

Muscat Water Ice: Infuse 4 large handfuls of balckcurrant leaves in the hot sugar and gelatine syrup (recipe p.3) for half an hour. Strain, squeezing the leaves well to extract the juice. Continue as for the basic recipe. Serve with melon.

Rhubarb and Orange: Stew 500mg/1lb rhubarb with the rind and juice of 2 oranges, until soft. Mash to a pulp. Add to the hot sugar and gelatine syrup mixture (recipe p.3). Continue as for the basic recipe.

SHERBETS

These are basically the same as sorbets, except that you add whipped cream instead of egg white.

Mango Sherbet: Stir 450ml/¾ pint mango purée (canned or fresh fruit purée) into 300ml/½ pint sugar syrup (recipe p.20). Freeze for 1 hour or until partially frozen. Turn into a bowl, and beat lightly. Whip 150ml/¼ pint double cream until it just holds its shape. Fold into sherbet and refreeze until firm.

Blackcurrant and Port Sherbet Make 300ml/½ pint blackcurrant fruit purée. Add to 300ml/½ pint sugar syrup (recipe p.20) with 2 tablespoons Ruby Port. Freeze for 1 hour or until partially frozen. Turn into a bowl, and beat lightly. Whip 150ml/¼ pint double cream until it just holds its shape. Fold into sherbet and refreeze until firm.

GRANITAS

Granitas are made from flavoured sugar syrups. If you are making granitas to serve on the same day, start about 3 hours before serving and stir the mixture frequently during freezing until the ice is slushy and mouth-watering. Serve scooped into long tall glasses. If you are making them to serve later, freeze the mixture without stirring. Let it thaw for 1 hour before serving, whisking it frequently with a fork to break up the crystals. Here are some suggestions:

COFFEE GRANITA
Serves 4–6

One for fresh coffee fanatics! Serve with a little rum and cream if liked.

4 tablespoons freshly ground medium roast coffee
500ml/1 pint water
150g/5oz muscovado sugar

Place coffee in a fine filter and pour boiling water through. Stir in sugar until dissolved. Cool, then freeze, stirring frequently until mushy. Serve in tall glasses.

KIR ROYALE GRANITA
Serves 6–8

Make this refreshing, wonderful dinner party dessert the day before you need it. It needs 1 day to freeze, yet it will never actually freeze solid. Just perfect for immediate serving.

4 tablespoons runny honey
300ml/½ pint inexpensive medium dry sparkling white wine
2 tablespoons cassis or blackcurrant liqueur

Place the honey in a saucepan with 150ml/¼ pint water. Bring to the boil and boil for 5 minutes. Cool. Stir in the wine and cassis. Freeze for at least 12 hours. Serve in tall glasses.

To Store
Cover tightly and keep container upright. Store for up to 2 weeks only. The flavour diminishes with longer freezing.

WATERMELON GRANITA

Very refreshing on a summer's day.

300ml/½ pint watermelon purée
150ml/¼ pint sugar syrup (recipe p.20)

Stir melon purée and sugar syrup together. Freeze, stirring frequently until mushy.

EARL GREY'S ICE

Refreshing and lemony. Try jasmine tea, too.

500ml/1 pint water
175g/6oz sugar
rind and juice of 2 lemons
2 tablespoons Earl Grey tea

Place water, sugar and lemon rind in a saucepan. Heat gently to dissolve sugar, then boil for 5 minutes. Remove from the heat and add the tea leaves. Let soak for 30 minutes, then strain. Add the lemon juice. Chill and freeze to a mush, stirring frequently with a fork to break up crystals.

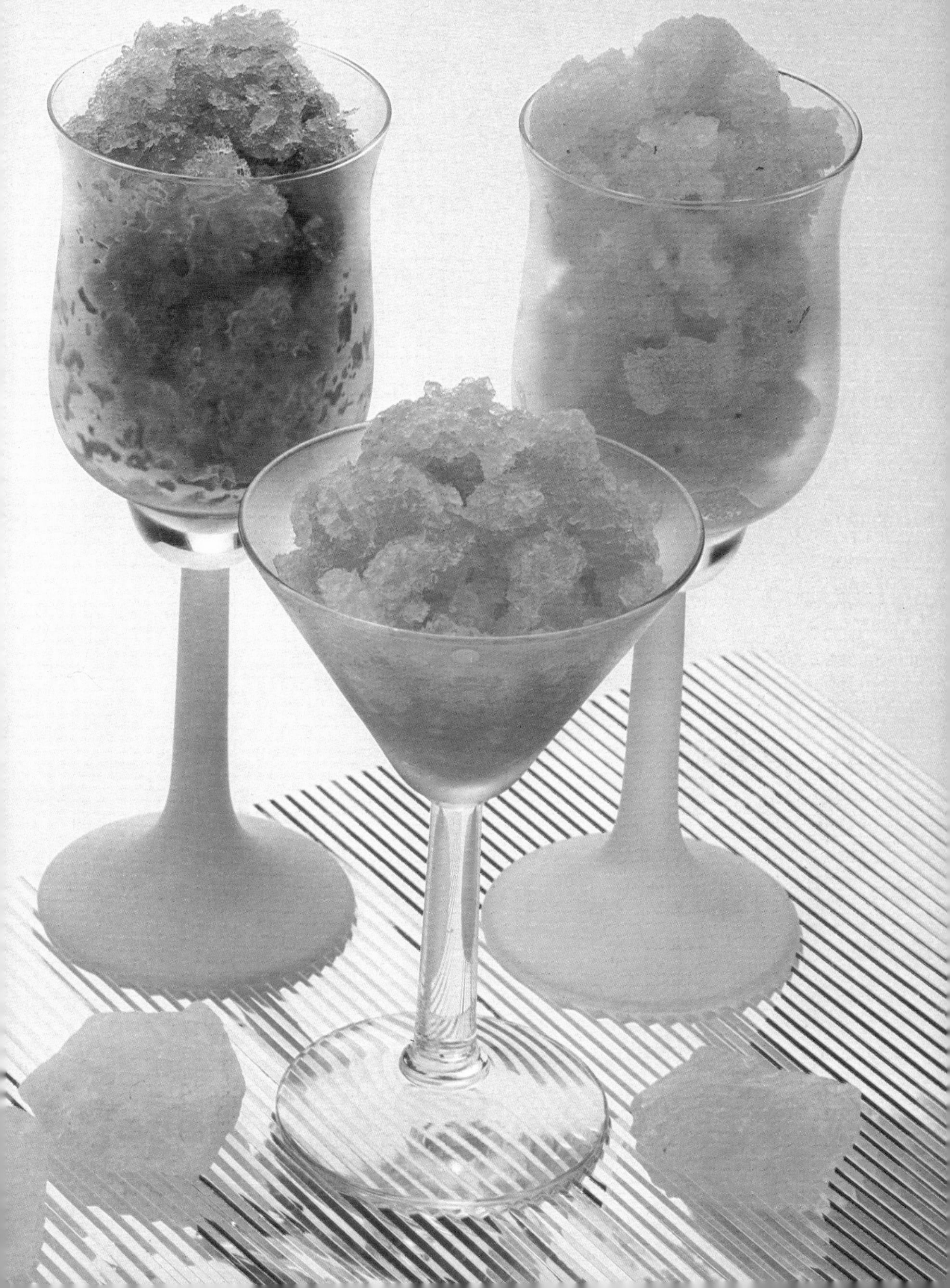

SAUCES

Jammy Ice Cream Sauce

Use "extra fruit" jams for a rich, fruity sauce; black cherry is especially good. Melt 4 tablespoons jam with 1 tablespoon lemon juice in a small pan. Sieve if desired. Allow to cool slightly. Serve warm. To serve cold, add 1 tablespoon water.

Marshmallow Sauce

Place 1 200-g/7.5-oz packet marshmallows with 4 tablespoons milk in a basin over a pan of hot but not boiling water. Stir until marshmallows have melted and sauce is smooth. Serve hot. For a change, try stirring in a little grated chocolate or desiccated coconut before serving.

Hot Butterscotch Sauce

100g/4oz light muscovado sugar
50g/2oz butter
4 tablespoons golden syrup

Place sugar, butter and syrup in a small pan. Stir over a low heat until ingredients are melted, then stir in 2 tablespoons water and remove from heat. Allow to cool slightly before serving.

Chocolate Dessert Sauce

Chocolate sauce is always a favourite. Why not make a large batch and divide it? Vary the flavour by adding a few drops of peppermint essence, 2 tablespoons orange marmalade, or 2 tablespoons peanut or hazelnut butter.

4 tablespoons cocoa powder
4 tablespoons golden syrup

Place cocoa powder and syrup in a small pan. Stir gently over a low heat until smooth. Bring to boil then remove from heat. Store in a covered container for up to 3 weeks. Serve cold.

LOLLIPOPS

To make lollipops you can use all kinds of containers. Yogurt and dessert cartons make rather large lollies but they keep the kids quiet for ages. Add lolly sticks when the mixture is almost frozen. Ice cube trays are also good; make two or three different flavours, tipping each one into a plastic bag to store when frozen, and then serve added to a milk drink. You can buy lolly sticks, lolly bags (plastic bags divided into long strips) and lolly moulds from major freezer centres.

Fruit and Yogurt Lollies: Whisk together equal quantities of natural yogurt and fruit juices until smooth and freeze. Or freeze commercial fruit juice and yogurt drink.

Fruit Purée Lollies: Stew fruit such as apple, rhubarb and blackberries with a little sugar, or simply purée soft fruits; then freeze.

MILK LOLLIES

The sugar and cornflour content is important to help achieve the smooth lip-licking texture that the children love.

600ml/1 pint milk
75g/3oz sugar
1 tablespoon cornflour flavouring: see below

Place 2 tablespoons of milk in a basin, add the sugar and cornflour, stir well. Heat remaining milk to just below boiling, stir onto the cornflour mixture and return to pan. Cook for a further 1 minute. Remove from heat and cool. Add flavouring. Pour into lolly moulds and freeze firm.

Banana: Mash 3 overripe bananas and stir into hot milk. Or add banana milk shake mix.

Milk Shake: Use only 2 tablespoons sugar and add 3 tablespoons milk shake concentrate to the cooled milk.

Chocolate: Omit sugar from recipe and stir 2–3 tablespoons chocolate drinking powder into milk with the cornflour. Sweeten if necessary.

Mint: Add only 1 tablespoon sugar and 2 tablespoons green mint-flavoured syrup.

Liquorice lollies: Melt 100g/4oz liquorice toffees in the milk and omit the sugar.

FRUIT COULIS

This simply means puréed fresh fruit sweetened with a little sugar or lemon juice if desired. Ideal fruits are strawberry, raspberry, black- and redcurrants, blackberries, kiwi fruit—in fact most fruits that can be pushed through a sieve (and muslin if you wish to remove tiny pips) to make a smooth, glossy sauce. Serve them with contrasting fresh fruits, ice creams and pastries.

ICE BOWL

A great presentation for fresh fruits. Fill a plastic or freezer proof glass bowl with water. Place a smaller bowl inside and weigh it down. Freeze for 2–3 hours then push slices of lemon, grapes or strawberries, or flower petals into the iced water. Allow to freeze all day until solid. Remove from freezer half an hour before serving and the two bowls should slip away from the ice.

FRESH CREAM CHOCOLATES

Makes 18–20

Use the gold or silver-foil-coated petits fours cases if you can find them, or use two paper ones put together to prevent collapsing. Grate 100g/4oz plain dark chocolate and melt in a basin over hot water. Using a pastry brush, coat the inside of paper cases. Chill, then repeat. To fill: place a piece of glacé cherry, pineapple or a little nut in each case. Lightly whip 150ml/¼ pint double cream until it just holds its shape. Stir in 2 teaspoons icing sugar. Divide cream between three bowls and to each one add 1–2 tablespoons (or to taste) of liqueur such as Grand Marnier, cherry brandy, crème de menthe, Amaretto. Place each in a small piping bag fitted with a 1-cm/¼-in plain tube and pipe a little into each case. Place remaining melted chocolate in a small greaseproof paper piping bag and snip end. Pipe chocolate over cream until completely covered. Top with a little cherry or nut. Allow to set.

These will keep for up to 5 days in the fridge.

ICE CREAM TRUFFLES

After-dinner sweets with a cool surprise. These are a bit fiddly, so don't try to make too many! Use home made or commercial ice cream.

Use a melon baller to make tiny scoops of ice cream (an assortment of flavours if possible). Freeze on a plastic tray until hard. Skewer on cocktail sticks then dip a couple at a time into a small bowl of Ice Magic Chocolate Topping—this is a commercial ice cream sauce that sets hard in seconds. Ordinary melted chocolate doesn't work. Then dip truffles in chocolate vermicelli or desiccated coconut. Freeze again. Serve frozen.

ICE CREAM CAKES AND DESSERTS

CHOC-MINT AND MALLOW BIRTHDAY CAKE
Serves 12

A fantastic centre piece for a birthday table. You can make this cake using any flavour of ice cream. And of course it won't go to waste—just put it back in the freezer!

CHOCOLATE CAKE

100g/4oz block margarine (at room temperature)
100g/4oz caster sugar
2 size 2 eggs
75g/3oz self-raising flour
25g/1oz cocoa powder
1 teaspoon baking powder

ICE CREAM

1 quantity Choc-chip ice cream (p.7)
1 quantity Marshmallow ice cream (p.7)

TO DECORATE

150ml/¼ pint double or whipping cream
chocolate buttons, 5 ice cream wafers

Set oven at 180°C/350°F/Gas 4. Grease and line one deep 20-cm/8-in round cake tin. Place all ingredients in a large bowl and beat together with a wooden spoon for 2–3 minutes until smooth. (This will take only 1–2 minutes in an electric mixer—do not over beat.) Spread mixture in tin and bake for 30–35 minutes. Cool on a wire rack. When cold split into

three layers. Remove ice creams from freezer to soften a little. Wash and grease and line the cake tin again. Place the base of the cake back into the tin. Scoop the Choc-chip ice cream over the cake, smoothing out any gaps and spreading the mixture up to the sides of the tin. Place another layer of cake on top. Scoop the marshmallow ice cream over and top with the last layer of cake. Press cake down well cover with foil and freeze until firm—for at least 3 hours.

To Serve and Decorate
Remove the cake from the freezer 1 hour before serving. Remove cake from tin and place on serving plate. Whip cream until it just holds its shape. Spread thinly over the top of cake. Cut ice cream wafers diagonally into triangles and arrange on cake, with chocolate buttons between.

ALPINE CHATEAU
Serves 6–8

Choose your own ice cream and cake flavours to complement each other; then freeze and slice for when you want a posh pud! This can be made with commercial soft-scoop ice cream, too.

FILLING
½ quantity Cherry and Kirsch meringue ice— made with red cherries (recipe p.13)

CAKE
Bake 1 Whisked sponge cake (recipe p.58) in a 28 × 17cm/11 × 7in swiss roll tin.

TO DECORATE
150ml/¼ pint double cream
4 maraschino or cocktail cherries on stalks

Make the ice cream or remove from freezer and allow to thaw in fridge for 10–15 minutes. Place the sponge

upside down on a serving plate or cake board. Place small scoops of ice cream widthways across the centre third of the cake, smoothing and piling it up in the centre. Press the sides of the cake up over the ice cream. Press to form a triangle. Cover tightly with cling film and freeze until firm.

To decorate: Remove dessert from freezer 1 hour before serving. Lightly whip cream until it just holds its shape. Place half in a nylon piping bag fitted with a star tube. Spread remaining over top and sides of dessert. Pipe swirls of cream on top and base of cake. Allow dessert to thaw in fridge for at least 30 minutes before serving. Or cut off one slice at a time and thaw for 15 minutes.

ICED CHESTNUT LOG
Serves 10

A spectacular dessert that's not difficult to make, this ice cream is firm enough to mould into shape, though it does need a little patience! Delicious served before freezing as a mousse too.

3 eggs, separated
496-g/17½-oz can sweetened chestnut purée
3 tablespoons rum
75g/3oz icing sugar
300ml/½ pint double cream

TO DECORATE
300ml/½ pint double cream
chocolate stars (see p.62)

Beat the egg yolks until pale and creamy, then beat in the chestnut purée, rum and sugar, beating with a wooden spoon until smooth. Lightly whip cream until it just holds its shape, and fold into chestnut mixture. Whisk egg whites until stiff but not dry, and fold in. Place in a container and freeze for 2 hours or until firm but not solid. Scoop ice cream into bowl; mash lightly then turn onto a sheet of foil. Fold foil tightly around mixture. Roll lightly into a sausage shape. Freeze until firm, occasionally rolling the mixture into a smooth shape. When firm remove foil and place ice cream on a serving plate. Place in fridge for 1 hour. Smooth ice cream into a smooth shape.

To decorate: Whip cream until it just holds its shape and place in a nylon piping bag fitted with a medium star tube. Pipe cream over dessert. Decorate with chocolate stars (recipe p.62).

CHEESECAKES

BAKED LEMON RAISIN CHEESECAKE

Serves 8

A traditional cheesecake, very thick and cheesy. Allow it to cool completely in the oven; don't worry if the top cracks slightly.

BASE
2 125-g/4½-oz packets shortbread biscuits
75g/3oz butter

FILLING
rind and juice of 1 lemon
225g/8oz cottage cheese
200g/7½oz full fat soft cheese
100g/4oz caster sugar
50g/2oz softened butter
3 size 3 eggs
75g/3oz raisins
3 tablespoons lemon juice (for glaze)
1 lemon, sliced

Set oven at 160°C/325°F/Gas 3. Line the base of a deep, 20-cm/8-in loose-based round cake tin with greaseproof paper. Place on a baking sheet. Crush biscuits. Melt butter in a small pan, stir in biscuits and press over base and half way up sides of cake tin. Chill. Press cottage cheese through a sieve into a bowl; add the soft cheese, **only** 50g/2oz caster sugar, and the softened butter. Beat until smooth. Gradually beat in the eggs, lemon rind and juice. Stir in raisins. Pour mixture in tin and bake in oven for 40–45 minutes until just set 3.5cm/1½in in from edge. The mixture will still be tacky, soft in the centre. Turn off oven and allow cheesecake to cool completely until set, overnight if possible.

Place lemon juice and remaining 50g/2oz sugar in a small pan with 3 tablespoons boiling water. Heat until sugar dissolves. Boil for 2–3 minutes. Cool slightly, then pour over cheesecake. Cut into wedges. Decorate with lemon slices. Freeze for up to 3 months.

STRAWBERRY ORANGE TERRINE
Serves 6–8

Serve surrounded by strawberry purée. Delicious in any fruit combination. Very posh!

**1 Whisked sponge cake (recipe p.58) baked in a
  28 × 18 cm/11 × 7 in tin**
150g/5oz low fat soft cheese
150ml/¼ pint double cream
2 oranges
3 teaspoons gelatine

1 egg white
2 tablespoons caster sugar
450g/11lb strawberries
icing sugar

Measure the sides, base and top of a 675-g/1½-lb loaf tin. Line tin with cling film. Cut the cake into oblong strips to fit the base and sides of the tin and reserve one strip of cake to seal over the top of the strawberry mixture. Grate the rind of 1 orange, cut in half and squeeze the juice. Cut peel and white pith from the remaining orange, and segment. Beat the cheese with the orange rind and caster sugar until smooth. Lightly whip the cream until it just holds its shape. Beat into the cheese mixture. Dissolve the gelatine in the orange juice and stir into the cheese mixture. Whisk the egg white until stiff but not dry. Fold into the mixture. Chill until mixture begins to thicken and set. Spoon half the mixture into the sponge lined loaf tin. Arrange whole strawberries down the length of the tin. Chop the orange segments, drain and scatter orange over the cheese mixture. Top with remaining cheese mixture and sponge cake. Press down well and chill until firm. Reserve eight whole strawberries, and press remaining through a sieve into a bowl. Mix with a little icing sugar. Invert dessert onto a serving plate and decorate with sliced strawberries. Served sliced with strawberry purée.

Freeze for up to 2 months. Defrost in fridge overnight.

BLACK- AND REDCURRANT CHEESECAKE

Serves 6–8

Looks and tastes stunning. Don't overcook the currants or they will be too mushy and wet. Canned, (drained) or frozen fruit can also be used.

225g/8oz sweetmeal biscuits
75g/3oz butter
2 tablespoons honey
225g/8oz redcurrants
225g/8oz blackcurrants
4 tablespoons sugar
300g/10oz low fat soft cheese
150ml/¼ pint sour cream
3 teaspoons gelatine
2 egg whites

Crush biscuits finely. Melt butter in a small pan; stir in honey and biscuits. Press onto base of a 20-cm/8-in loose-bottomed cake tin. String the black- and redcurrants; place in a small pan with 1 tablespoon water and 1 tablespoon sugar. Cook for 3 minutes; cool completely. Beat cheese with remaining sugar until smooth. Gradually beat in sour cream. Dissolve gelatine in 3 tablespoons water (see p.3) and stir into the cheese mixture with half of the fruit. Whisk egg whites until stiff but not dry; fold into the cheese mixture. Spread in tin and chill until firm, at least 2 hours. Remove sides of tin. Top with remaining fruit.

CHEESE & YOGURT DESSERTS

YOGURT MOUSSE

Serves 6

Very attractive—yet no more fattening than a carton of yogurt. Use a fruit-flavoured one as the natural yogurt does not taste good in this recipe. Serve with fruit coulis (p.26) if liked.

450ml/¾ pint fruit-flavoured yogurt, ie.
 strawberry, peach, rhubarb, redcurrant etc.
3 teaspoons gelatine
2 egg whites

Place the yogurt into a large bowl. Dissolve the gelatine in 3 tablespoons cold water (see p.3) and beat into yogurt. Allow to cool until on the point of setting. Whisk egg whites until stiff but not dry and fold into yogurt. Pour into individual greased moulds or glass dishes and allow to set. Decorate with fresh fruit or serve with a fruit coulis.

Whole Fruit Yogurt Mousse: Soak 225g/8oz mixed dried fruit such as figs, dates, prunes, apples, apricots in 300ml/½ pint cold tea. Soak overnight then blend in a liquidiser or food processor until smooth. Fold into yogurt with egg whites.

APRICOT QUARK DESSERT

Serves 6

Quark is a Continental-style skimmed milk soft cheese, it's a natural, healthy compliment to fruit. Look for it in chill cabinets of the supermarket.

411-g/14-oz can apricot halves in natural juices
2 teaspoons gelatine
200-g/7-oz tub plain Quark or low fat soft
 cheese
1 tablespoon light soft brown sugar, or to taste
2 egg whites

Drain apricots, placing juice in a small bowl, sprinkle gelatine over and dissolve (see p.3). Finely chop or purée apricots. Stir into juice and spoon into individual serving dishes, reserving a little for decoration. Whisk the Quark and sugar until smooth; gradually beat in the gelatine. Chill until on the point of setting. Whisk egg whites until stiff but not dry. Fold into Quark mixture; sweeten to taste. Pour onto apricots. Decorate with remaining chopped fruit.

GREEK YOGURT WITH HONEY
Serves 4

A light dessert at the end of a meal. This is deliciously simple and very "more-ish"—the grated lemon and orange rinds are well worth adding.

4 tablespoons runny honey
1 teaspoon grated lemon rind
1 teaspoon grated orange rind
1 tablespoon orange juice
1 pint natural yogurt
50g/2oz toasted, flaked almonds

Mix the honey, grated rind and fruit juice together. Gradually stir in the yogurt and chill. Sprinkle with toasted almonds.

COEUR À LA CRÈME
Serves 6

This cheese and cream confection is traditionally made in heart-shaped moulds which have draining holes in the bottom. These are expensive and rather a luxury, but this method works just as well. **You will need to start 2 days before serving.**

225g/8oz cottage cheese
300ml/½ pint double cream
2 tablespoons caster sugar
2 egg whites
250g/8oz strawberries
2 tablespoons Kirsch or cherry liqueur

Line the base of six small ramekin dishes with a little greased greaseproof paper. Grease sides of dishes. Push the cottage cheese through a sieve, into a bowl. Stir in the double cream and sugar to taste. Whisk the egg whites until stiff but not dry and fold into the cheese mixture. Divide between ramekin dishes. Cover tightly with cling film. Prick the cling film well with a cocktail stick. Cover a wire cooling rack with kitchen paper and turn the ramekin dishes upside down onto the rack. Leave in a cool place for two days to allow a little moisture to drain away. Remove cling film, run a knife around dessert and invert onto serving plates.

Thinly slice six strawberries for decoration. Press remaining through a sieve. Add liqueur and sweeten with a little icing sugar if liked. Pour sauce around dessert and decorate with strawberries. Serve chilled.

FRESH FRUIT IDEAS

PEACH, MELON AND GINGER SALAD

Place the juice from 1 small can of peaches in natural juices into a small pan with the shredded rind and juice of 1 orange and 3 pieces of stem ginger, sliced. Add one tablespoon of the syrup from the ginger jar; stir in 1 teaspoon cornflour and bring to the boil. Cook for 1 minute. Cool. Scoop melon balls from one small honeydew melon and arrange on individual plates with the peach slices. Pipe a thin line of sieved raspberry jam around the fruits and pour a little syrup just inside the line.

ORANGE, CRANBERRY AND PERNOD SUNBURST

Stew 225g/8oz cranberries (or redcurrants) in a little water with enough sugar to sweeten (about 3 tablespoons) until just tender. Cool. Using a sharp knife, cut off all peel and white pith from 4 oranges. Slice oranges and arrange on individual plates. Place cranberries or redcurrants in centre and scatter with walnut halves. Pour 1 teaspoon of Pernod over each. Serve chilled.

CARIBBEAN COCKTAIL

Fresh lime juice makes this cocktail really tangy, but you could use 4 tablespoons of lime cordial to make the syrup—and omit 50g/2oz of sugar from the recipe.

225g/8oz sugar
2 limes, or 3 tablespoons lime juice
2 mangoes
4 bananas
225g/8oz fresh dates

Dissolve sugar in 300ml/½ pint water over a low heat. Cool. Add the grated rind and juice of 1 lime. Thinly slice the remaining lime. Cut the mangoes lengthways, either side of the long flat central stone. Cut flesh into strips and cut off skin. Add to syrup with the lime slices. Peel and slice bananas, and halve and stone the dates. Add to the syrup. Serve chilled.

SUMMER PUDDING
Serves 6

A traditional British pudding and an ideal dessert to freeze—to capture the taste of summer.

8 thick slices white bread from a large loaf
750g/1½lb mixed fruits: blackcurrants,
** redcurrants, strawberries, blackberries or**
** raspberries**
100g/4oz granulated sugar
cream to serve

Remove crusts from bread and line side and base of a 900-ml/1-½ pint pudding basin with six slices of bread, trimming to fit where necessary; slightly overlap slices lining the side. Strip blackcurrants and redcurrants from stalks, if used; hull strawberries, if used. Place 2 tablespoons water and sugar in a saucepan; dissolve sugar over a low heat. Reserve some whole fruits for decoration; add remainder to saucepan. Cover; stew gently for 5 minutes or until soft, being careful not to break the fruit too much. Pour mixture into lined pudding basin; cover with remaining slices of bread, trimming to fit. Cover with a saucer or small plate and place a weight on top. Leave to cool, then chill overnight in refrigerator. Invert onto a serving plate, decorate top of the pudding with reserved fruit and serve with cream.

Freeze until firm, then remove from basin, wrap in freezer film and freeze for up to 6 months.

MIDDLE EASTERN DRIED FRUIT SALAD
Serves 6–8

This is a wonderful winter pud, especially served with yogurt. Great for breakfast too!

750g/1½lb mixed dried fruits, prunes, apple
** rings, pears, figs, apricots and peach**
4 tablespoons honey
1 cinnamon stick
3 teaspoons triple-strength rose-water
25g/1oz pistachio nuts
25g/1oz pine nuts

Wash dried fruits, then soak in cold water overnight. Measure the water the following morning, make up to 600ml/1 pint if necessary. Place water, honey, cinnamon stick and fruit together in a pan; simmer for 20 minutes until tender. Cool slightly. Remove cinnamon stick. Add rose water and nuts, stir well, serve warm or cold.

CHERRY COMPOTE
Serves 4–6

The most delicious way to serve fresh cherries. Serve with clotted cream, or pour over ice cream.

2 oranges
450g/1lb cherries
50g/2oz sugar
4 tablespoons port or red wine
4 tablespoons redcurrant jelly
2–3 teaspoons cornflour

Using a sharp knife or potato peeler, pare rind from oranges taking care not to include white pith. Cut rind into long thin strips. Cut oranges in half, and squeeze juice. Stone cherries, place in a pan with sugar, port or wine, orange rind and juice and redcurrant jelly. Bring to the boil. Reduce heat and simmer for 3 minutes. Mix cornflour with 2 tablespoons cold water, stir into cherry mixture, cook for a further 2 minutes until smooth. Cool, serve chilled.

Freeze for up to 6 months. Defrost in fridge for 6 hours.

CHEESECAKE TRUFFLES
Served with fresh fruit
Makes 12

Fresh fruit often needs a little creaminess, so try these lemon and coconut flavoured cream-cheese truffles with it, and just arrange beautifully on a plate.

175g/6oz low fat soft cream cheese
grated rind and juice of 1 lemon
sugar
50g/2oz dessicated coconut, toasted

Beat the cheese with the rind of the lemon, and a little sugar to taste. Roll teaspoonfulls of mixture in coconut and chill. Serve with the lemon juice and sliced fresh fruits such as mango, pineapple, figs, dates, melon balls, or whole raspberries.

APPLE AND ORANGE TEMPTATION

Serves 4

Make sure you choose firm, crisp eating apples such as Golden Delicious or Granny Smiths for this fresh-tasting instant dessert.

50g/2oz hazelnuts
2 green eating apples
2 oranges
300ml/½ pint natural yogurt
4 tablespoons muscovado sugar

Toast the hazelnuts under a hot grill until the skins begin to flake off. Place nuts in a teatowel and rub off skins. Finely chop nuts. Coarsely grate the apples, discarding cores. Grate orange rind and stir into yogurt. Cut peel and white pith from orange; segment fruit. Layer apple, orange, sugar and yogurt together in individual glasses. Top with nuts and serve chilled, within 2 or 3 hours.

PINEAPPLE AND PASSION FRUIT CUP

If you've never tried these unusual fruits, this is the combination to convert you!

1 small pineapple
1 312-g/11-oz can lychees or 250g/½lb fresh
1 pomegranate
2 passion fruits
2 fresh figs
2 tablespoons rum or Bacardi

Cut pineapple in half lengthways. Score down through the centre, and run a sharp knife around sides to loosen flesh from pineapple shell. Scoop out flesh and chop into small triangles, removing any woody core. Mix pineapple with lychees and juice. Cut pomegranate in half, scoop out seeds, taking care not to include any pith. Cut passion fruits in half and scoop out seeds. Slice figs. Mix all the fruits together with rum or Bacardi. Chill. Serve piled back into the pineapple shell.

TRIFLES, SYLLABUBS AND FOOLS

CARIBBEAN TRIFLE

Ginger, pineapple, coconut and bananas make up this wonderful trifle.

3 tablespoons custard powder
2 tablespoons sugar
600ml/1 pint milk
2 bananas
1 Jamaica Ginger Cake
1 400-g/14-oz can pineapple rings in natural juice
2 tablespoons coconut-flavoured liqueur or rum
150ml/¼ pint double whipping cream
2 150-g/5.29-oz cartons pineapple and coconut-flavoured yogurt
toasted coconut to decorate

Make custard. Blend powder and sugar with a little cold milk. Bring remaining milk to the boil; pour onto custard and mix well. Return to saucepan and bring to the boil. Slice bananas into custard. Remove from heat and leave to cool. (Cover with a circle of damp greaseproof paper to prevent a skin forming.) Cut cake into slices and arrange in the base of a large serving bowl. Drain juice from pineapple; mix half with liqueur or rum if used, and pour over the cake. Reserve 4 pineapple rings. Chop remainder into pieces and place over cake. Pour over the cooled custard and leave to set. Lightly whip the cream until it just holds its shape. Fold in the yogurt and swirl it over the custard. Decorate with remaining pineapple slices, sliced banana, and toasted coconut.

OLD ENGLISH SHERRY TRIFLE

Serves 6–8

A rich and luxurious trifle, made in the traditional way with a soft egg custard on top. If you're in a hurry, use a can of custard.

225g/8oz madeira cake
raspberry jam
50g/2oz ratafia biscuits OR
3 large macaroons
150ml/¼ pint sweet sherry
225/8oz grapes
4 egg yolks
2 tablespoons flour
600ml/1 pint milk
50g/2oz caster sugar
150ml/¼ pint double cream
glacé cherries and ratafia biscuits to decorate

Cut cake into slices and spread thickly with jam. Place in the bottom of a trifle dish with crushed biscuits or macaroons. Halve and pip grapes. Place over cake. Pour sherry over cake.

To make custard: Beat egg yolks and flour together. Heat milk and sugar in a pan, until warm but not boiling. Stir into egg yolks. Return to pan and cook over a gentle heat, stirring constantly until thickened. Pour over sponge. Leave in cool place to set. Whip cream until it just holds its shape. Swirl over trifle with a palette knife. Roughly chop cherries; scatter over trifle and arrange biscuits around edge of dish.

ZABAGLIONE

This classic Italian dessert takes only minutes to make, so prepare the ingredients before the meal and whisk together at the last moment. It will separate if kept waiting long.

FOR EACH PORTION

1 teaspoon flaked almonds
1 egg yolk
1 teaspoon caster sugar
1 tablespoon sherry or sweet vermouth

Prepare a medium grill. Lightly toast the almonds until golden. Reserve. Place the egg yolk, sugar and sherry or vermouth in a basin. Just before serving, place basin over a saucepan of hot, not boiling, water. Whisk mixture continuously until thick and fluffy. Remove bowl from saucepan. Pour mixture into a tall glass. Sprinkle with toasted almonds, and serve at once.

TRADITIONAL WINE SYLLABUB
Serves 6

Prepare the ingredients ahead, and then make this dessert minutes before serving. It's very quick. For an everlasting syllabub, omit the egg white.

300ml/½ pint double cream
75g/3oz caster sugar
2 tablespoons lemon juice
150ml/¼ pint sweet white wine
OR sherry and brandy mixed
2 egg whites

Whip the cream until it just holds its shape; whisk in the sugar, lemon juice and wine, or sherry and brandy. Whisk the egg whites until stiff but not dry and fold into the cream. Pour into glasses. Serve chilled, topped with strips of lemon rind.

MANGO AND GINGER FOOL
Serves 4–6

Quick and simple to make, this fool won't separate.

2 eggs, separated
75g/3oz icing sugar
150ml/¼ pint double cream
1 large ripe mango
2 tablespoons lemon juice
4 pieces preserved stem ginger in syrup OR
4 tablespoons ginger preserve–jam
For decoration: a little plain chocolate, grated

Place egg whites and icing sugar in a large mixing bowl. Using an electric mixer, whisk until very thick and creamy, like meringue. The mixture should stand in soft peaks. This may take up to 10 minutes. (Alternatively, whisk by hand over a saucepan of hot water.) Lightly whip cream until it just holds its shape; fold into the egg whites with the egg yolks. Cut mango in half, down both sides of the flat stone. Scoop out flesh and purée in a liquidiser, or chop very finely. Fold into the mixture with the lemon juice. Slice ginger thinly and stir into dessert, or stir in jam. Divide between glasses. Chill and serve topped with chocolate.

GOOSEBERRY AND ELDERFLOWER FOOL
Serves 6

It's always worth making the most of fruits when they are in season. If you live in the country, why not pick fresh elderflowers to give this dessert a delicately perfumed flavour; they turn this simple dessert into something quite special.

450g/1lb gooseberries (fresh or frozen and thawed)
1–2 tablespoons sugar to taste
6 heads of elderflowers
150ml/¼ pint custard
150ml/¼ pint double or whipping cream, whipped

Place the gooseberries, 2 tablespoons water and the elderflowers in a small pan. Cook for 5–10 minutes until tender. Remove elderflowers. Reserve 18 whole gooseberries for decoration; press the remaining through a nylon sieve. Cool. Fold custard, cream and fruit purée together. Serve in individual glasses topped with fruit.

You can use any puréed fruit: rhubarb, apricot, blackberry, apple, raspberry. Add sugar to taste.

Another alternative is to use 300ml/½ pint double cream instead of custard.

APPLE SNOW
Serves 4

Light and refreshing, this is an ideal last minute dessert, especially if you have canned or frozen apple purée at hand.

300ml/½ pint apple purée, made from 450g/1lb cooking apples, fresh or frozen, or a can of apple purée
2 teaspoons lemon juice
2 eggs

Taste apple purée and sweeten if desired. Separate eggs; add yolks and lemon juice to apple purée and stir well. Place whites in a clear, grease-free bowl and whisk until stiff but not dry. Fold into apples and chill until ready to serve.

SOFT SOUFFLÉS

THE CLASSIC SOUFFLÉ

Serves 6

Lemon soufflé is always a favourite—try other citrus flavours, or fruit soufflés too. Use strong flavours that will come through the cream and egg mixture.

To make Chocolate Soufflé Collars, see note at end of recipe.

LEMON, ORANGE OR LIME

4 eggs, separated
100g/4oz caster sugar
rind and juice of 2½ lemons OR 2 oranges OR 3
  limes
4 teaspoons gelatine
300ml/½ pint double cream

FRUIT PURÉE

4 eggs, separated
50g/2oz caster sugar
300ml/½ pint fruit purée (apricot,
  blackcurrant, raspberry, sweetened to taste)
4 teaspoons gelatine
150ml/¼ pint double cream
3 tablespoons fruit flavoured liqueur—such as
  Cherry or apricot brandy

Prepare a 15-cm/6-in 900-ml/1½-pint soufflé dish or mould. Wrap a double strip of greaseproof paper around dish, to stand 5cm/2in above dish. Tie with string or secure with sticky tape. Grease paper with a little oil. Place the egg yolks, and sugar in a bowl with the citrus rind and juice or the fruit purée. Place bowl over a pan of hot but not boiling water. The pan should not touch the water. Whisk at high speed until the mixture becomes thick, creamy and mousse-like. The mixture should leave a definite trail when the whisk is lifted. Lightly whip cream until it just holds its shape.

Dissolve gelatine in 3 tablespoons water (see p.3); add to fruit mixture, whisking continuously. Fold in the cream and liqueur if used. Whisk egg whites until stiff but not dry and fold into mixture using a large metal spoon. Chill the bowl of mixture for a few minutes until it begins to thicken, then pour it into prepared dish. Chill until set. Carefully ease the paper away from the mixture with a knife dipped in hot water. Decorate the top with extra piped cream and fruit or chopped nuts.

Chocolate Collars:
Melt 175g/6oz plain cooking chocolate with 15g/½oz butter and 1 tablespoon water; spread around inside of greaseproof collars, allow to set, then peel off paper.

PEACH BANANA SOUFFLÉ

Soufflés are not just for special occasions. This one is so simple you could make a different version every day. Use real fruit jellies for the best flavour.

FOR 4–6 PORTIONS

150-g/6-oz can evaporated milk
1 packet peach jelly
300ml/½ pint boiling water
3 bananas
150-ml/5-fl oz carton peach melba-flavoured
** yogurt**
banana chips to decorate

Wrap a band of double-thickness greaseproof paper around the outside of a 750-ml/1½-pint shallow 15-cm/6-in soufflé dish, so that it stands 5cm/2in above rim. Secure tightly with string or sticky tape. Pour evaporated milk into a large bowl and then place in refrigerator. Dissolve the jelly in boiling water. Cool, then place in refrigerator until just beginning to set. Whisk evaporated milk until thick creamy and mousse-like. Gradually whisk in the partially-set jelly. Peel and mash the bananas with the yogurt. Whisk the two into the jelly mixture, until blended. Pour into prepared soufflé dish. Chill for at least two hours or until set. To serve, remove the tape or string and peel paper from dish, using the back of a knife to hold edge. Decorate with banana chips.

CHOCOLATE CREATIONS

RICH CHOCOLATE FONDUE
Serves 6

Rather like a fresh fruit salad with a wicked rich chocolate sauce, this goes quite a long way but is not as extravagant as it sounds.

225g/8oz plain dark (or milk) chocolate
150ml/¼ pint double cream
2 tablespoons liqueur, brandy or rum

Break up chocolate and place in a small pan with 4 tablespoons cream and stir over a very low heat until chocolate has melted and mixture becomes smooth. Add liqueur and pour into a fondue pot or small bowl. Swirl remaining cream into fondue just before serving. Store in an airtight container in refrigerator for up to two weeks. Reheat as required. Serve with fresh fruit such as peaches, orange segments, cubed mango, fresh stoned dates, sliced bananas or strawberries. Place on cocktail sticks ready for dunking.

SOUR CREAM AND CHOCOLATE MOUSSE
Serves 4

The sour cream compliments the bitter chocolate perfectly in this light mousse. Use fresh cream if you prefer, and add a tablespoon of rum or brandy.

100g/4oz plain chocolate, grated
2 eggs, separated
150ml/¼ pint carton soured cream

Place chocolate in a basin over a saucepan of hot, but not boiling water, stirring occasionally, until chocolate has melted. Remove basin from saucepan. Add egg yolks to chocolate, beat until smooth. Whip cream until it just holds its shape; stir 4 tablespoons into chocolate until smooth. Whisk egg whites until stiff, but not dry. Using a metal spoon, fold into chocolate. Divide mixture between four individual glasses and chill until set. Divide remaining soured cream between glasses, and swirl on centre of mousse.

TRUFFLE TRIANGLES
Serves 10

A variation on the no-cook chocolate cake. Serve this sliced very thinly—it's very rich.

225g/8oz mixed dried fruit
2 tablespoons rum
125g/5oz plain cooking chocolate
50g/2oz butter
75g/3oz sweetmeal digestive biscuits
25g/1oz icing sugar
150ml/¼ pint whipped cream

Soak dried fruit in a basin with rum for 2–3 hours or overnight. Grate chocolate and place in a basin with butter over hot water until melted. Break biscuits into small pieces and stir into chocolate with mixed fruit and icing sugar. Stir until mixture is well coated with chocolate. Turn mixture down the centre of a large sheet of cling film or foil. Fold up sides and press into a triangle shape. Twist ends to secure and chill pudding in refrigerator until firm. Unwrap and serve cut into slices with whipped cream. It will keep in the fridge for up to 1 week.

To Freeze: Freeze without cream; wrapped in freezer film it will keep for up to 3 months.

CHOCOLATE ORANGE ROULADE

Serves 8

This ultimate chocolate swiss roll will cook with a sugary crust, with a sticky, uncooked appearance below. Don't worry; that is the secret of success. You will need to start this recipe 1 day before serving so that the crust softens and the whole cake can be rolled around lashings of cream.

1 tablespoon coffee granules
100g/4oz plain dark chocolate
4 large eggs, separated
100g/4oz caster sugar
300ml/½ pint double cream
rind of 1 orange
icing sugar to dust

Set oven to 180°C/350°F/Gas 4. Grease a 27 × 33cm/ 11 × 13in swiss roll tin. Cut a piece of non-stick baking parchment 5cm/2in bigger all around than tin. Fold up 2.5cm/1in all round. Snip into corners, press paper in tin and secure edges with paper clips. Blend the coffee to a smooth paste with 1 tablespoon water. Melt chocolate and cool slightly. Whisk egg yolks and sugar for 1 minute until thick and pale. Stir in the cool coffee and melted chocolate. Using a metal spoon, carefully fold in the stiffly-whisked egg whites. Spread into the prepared tin. Bake in centre of oven for about 15 minutes. The roulade will have a firm, crisp crust—do not break this—and the mixture beneath will seem very moist. Remove from oven. Cover lightly with a tea towel. Leave overnight for the crust to soften.

Whip cream until it just holds its shape, stir in orange rind. Place a large sheet of greaseproof paper on work surface and sprinkle thickly with icing sugar. Remove tea towel from tin. Flip roulade onto sugared paper. Trim off edges of roulade; carefully spread whipped cream over. Roll up roulade from one short end using the greaseproof paper to lift and roll. Place on serving plate and dust with icing sugar. Serve sliced.

CHOCOLATE HAZELNUT CHEESECAKE

Serves 6

Equally good as a mousse served in individual dishes or even as a nutty creamy filling for chocolates.

225g/8oz chocolate chip and hazelnut cookies
75g/3oz butter
225g/8oz curd cheese
4 rounded tablespoons chocolate and hazelnut flavour spread
300ml/½ pint double or whipping cream
2 teaspoons gelatine
2 egg whites

Crush the biscuits finely. Melt the butter in a small pan. Stir in the biscuit crumbs and press on the base of a greased 20-cm/8-in square loose-bottom cake tin. Chill. Beat cheese and chocolate hazelnut flavour spread together until smooth. Whip cream until it just holds its shape. Beat half the cream into the chocolate mixture. Dissolve gelatine in 3 tablespoons water (see p.3) and stir into mixture. Whisk egg whites until stiff but not dry and fold into chocolate mixture. Pour into tin and spread remaining cream lightly over to give a rippled effect. Chill until set.

To serve: Run a wet knife around the edge of tin and remove tin.

WHITE CHOCOLATE CREAMS

Serves 6

170–g/6–oz can evaporated milk
150–g/5–oz bar white chocolate, grated
3 teaspoons gelatine
300ml/½ pint double cream
2 egg whites
3 tablespoons coconut-flavoured liqueur OR rum (optional)
Chocolate stars (see p.62)
Chocolate dessert sauce (see p.24)

Grease six individual dariole or jelly moulds. Place the milk and chocolate in a saucepan. Heat gently until chocolate melts. Dissolve gelatine in 3 table-spoons cold water (see p.3). Stir into chocolate and allow mixture to cool. Whip cream until it just holds its shape. Whisk egg whites until stiff but not dry. Fold cream, egg whites and liqueur into chocolate mixture. Divide between moulds and chill until firm.

To serve: Dip moulds in hot water for a few seconds and invert onto individual plates. Decorate with chocolate stars and pour the dessert sauce over at the very last minute.

MERINGUE MAGIC

MERINGUES

This meringue should stay white, crisp and powdery. Ideal for fine shapes, it keeps in an airtight tin for weeks.

4 egg whites
100g/4oz caster sugar
100g/4oz icing sugar
15g/½oz cornflour

Set oven at 110°C/225°F/Gas ¼—or its lowest setting. Line three baking trays with non stick baking parchment. Whisk the egg whites until stiff but not dry. Add the caster sugar, whisking until the mixture is smooth and glossy. Sieve the icing sugar and cornflour together and fold into meringue with a metal spoon. Place in a nylon piping bag fitted with a plain or star tube and pipe meringue daisies, hearts or garlands onto baking trays. Bake for 1 hour or until firm. The meringues should lift away from the paper. Leave to dry in the oven overnight.

For Meringue Honey Pots:
Wrap three layers of foil half way round a small orange, apple or round object. Press foil tightly to make a smooth semi-circular mould. Slip foil mould off and stand them on a sheet of greaseproof paper, placed on a wire rack (checking that it will fit the oven). The hot air can then circulate under the meringue. Pipe the meringue around the mould, gradually building up meringue to cover it. Bake for 1½ hours and leave to dry completely. Ease out the foil moulds, and line the meringues with melted chocolate if desired. Fill with ice cream and fresh fruit, or with chocolate-flavoured cream or mousse.

CHOCOLATE MERINGUES

Makes 15 pairs

These meringues make wonderful petits fours, or a luxury dessert filled with almond-flavoured cream. The meringues can be made up to 3 weeks in advance and stored in a tin.

4 egg whites
225g/8oz caster sugar
100g/4oz plain dark chocolate, finely grated
150ml/¼ pint double cream
1 tablespoon almond liqueur

Set oven at 140°C/275°F/Gas 1. Line two baking sheets with non-stick baking parchment. Whisk egg whites until stiff but not dry. Whisk in 1 tablespoon sugar then, using a metal spoon, fold in remainder with the grated chocolate. Place mixture into a nylon piping bag fitted with a 1.5-cm/½-in plain tube. Pipe 20 fingers of meringue onto prepared baking sheet. Bake for 1½ hours or until dry and crisp. Lightly whip cream until it just holds its shape and fold in the liqueur. Sandwich the meringues in pairs with cream. Place in paper cases.

Serve within 1–2 hours.

PAVLOVA

Serves 8–10

The vinegar and cornflour give this meringue its soft, sticky centre and crisp exterior. A devastating dessert for dinner parties—it's never refused!

4 egg whites
¼ teaspoon salt
225g/8oz caster sugar
4 teaspoons cornflour
2 teaspoons vinegar
½ teaspoon vanilla flavouring
300ml/½ pint double cream, whipped
fresh fruit for filling

Set the oven at 140°C/275°F/Gas 1. Line a baking tray with non-stick baking parchment. Draw a 20-cm/8-in circle on paper. Place the egg whites in a clean, greasefree bowl; whisk until stiff but not dry. Add the sugar 1 tablespoon at a time, whisking until very stiff and glossy. Whisk in the cornflour, vinegar and vanilla. Spread mixture onto prepared baking tray and bake in heated oven for 1¼–1½ hours. Turn off oven and leave to cool in oven.

Fill with double cream, or Crème patissière (see recipe p.58) and fresh fruit.

PASTRY PERFECTIONS

FRENCH FLAN PASTRY

This is a crisp, sweet pastry base; like shortbread, it must be kneaded together. Sufficient for 20-cm/8-in flan case or 4–6 individual cases.

125g/5oz plain flour
75g/3oz butter, softened
50g/2oz caster sugar
1 egg yolk mixed with 1 tablespoon water

Place the flour in a bowl and make a well in the centre. Cut butter into small pieces, place in well with sugar and egg yolk. Using the fingers draw the flour into the butter and egg, mixing until well blended. (Alternatively, blend ingredients in a food processor. Turn out, knead until smooth.) Bake according to recipe. Freeze for up to 1 month, or bake and keep (unfilled) for up to 2 weeks in a tin.

TARTE AUX FRUIT
Serves 6

This recipe can be used for any fruit filling. For a classic apple tarte just top with sliced dessert apples, or use a combination of fresh or canned fruits.

1 quantity French flan pastry
450g/1lb cooking apples (about 2 medium)
a knob of butter
1 tablespoon sugar
1 dessert apple
6 victoria plums
6 apricots
2 tablespoons apricot jam

Set oven at 250°C/400°F/Gas 6. Roll out pastry and use to line a 18 × 28 cm/7 × 11 in flan tin. Chill. Meanwhile peel, core and slice cooking apples. Place in a small pan with butter, 1 tablespoon of water and sugar. Cover and cook over a low heat until the apples fall to a pulp. Cool. Cut dessert apples in half. Remove core with a teaspoon and cut into thin slices keeping the apple in its shape. Halve plums, removing stones; and halve apricots, removing stones. Place apple purée into pastry case. Arrange fruits on top. Warm and sieve apricot jam. Brush over the fruit and bake for 25–30 minutes until golden. Serve hot or cold.

FRUIT FLOWER POTS

Line six to eight 8-cm/3-in individual deep-dish bun or mince pie tins with French flan pastry (see recipe above). Bake at 190°C/375°F/Gas 5, for 15 minutes until golden. Leave in tin for 10 minutes, turn out and leave to cool. Fill the base with a little chopped fresh fruit such as strawberries, pineapple, kiwi fruit, grapes or jam, and top with Crème patissière (see p.58) or fresh whipped cream. Decorate with an arrangement of fruit. Glaze with a little warm apricot jam if desired.

TARTE AUX CITRON
Serves 6–8

Soft and tangy: even if you haven't a sweet tooth you'll find this very "more-ish." Bake the pastry case in advance to save time. The whole tarte will keep well for up to 3 days.

1 quantity French flan pastry (see recipe above)
50g/2oz butter
3 size 3 eggs, beaten
175g/6oz caster sugar
grated rind and juice of 2 lemons
grated rind and juice of 1 orange

TO DECORATE

50g/2oz sugar
1 lemon, sliced
1 orange, sliced

Set oven at 190°C/375°F/Gas 5. Line a 22-cm/8½-in fluted flan tin with the pastry. Line with greaseproof paper and baking beans (or rice). Bake "blind" for 10 minutes. Remove paper and beans and cook for a further 5 minutes. Melt the butter and beat in the eggs, sugar, fruit juice and rind. Pour into pastry case and bake for a further 20–25 minutes until just set. Place sugar and 300ml/½ pint water in a frying pan. Dissolve over a low heat. Add the sliced fruit to the pan. Simmer gently until the fruit is tender and the syrup is thick and sticky. Arrange on tarte and allow to cool.

MARMALADE AND COCONUT MILLE FEUILLE

Serves 6–8

A luxury dessert that's not as difficult to make as you may think. Follow the basic pastry structure for any fruit and cream filling.

375-g/13-oz packet frozen puff pastry, just thawed
300ml/½ pint milk
50g/2oz coconut
1½ tablespoons custard powder
1 tablespoon caster sugar
300ml/½ pint double cream
6 mandarin oranges, satsumas or clementines
3 tablespoons orange marmalade

Set oven at 230°C/450°F/Gas 8. Roll out pastry thickly and trim to an oblong 23 × 13cm/9 × 5in. Place on a wet baking sheet and prick well with a fork. Bake just above the centre of the oven for 10–15 minutes until well risen and golden brown. Remove from oven. Carefully split into three layers and trim edges with a sharp knife. Cool on a wire rack. Reserve 2 tablespoons of milk and heat the remaining. Stir in the coconut. Leave for 10 minutes then pour milk through a sieve into another saucepan. Press coconut well to squeeze out all the milk. Mix the 2 tablespoons of milk with the custard powder and sugar; add to hot milk; stir well and cook for 2 minutes until thickened. Cover closely and allow to cool. Whip cream until it just holds its shape; reserve half and fold remainder into the cold custard. Slice one mandarin or orange thinly and reserve for decoration. Peel, and segment remaining.

To Assemble: Reserve the bottom flattest layer of pastry for the top, and place the top layer of pastry as the base on a serving plate. Place fruit segments on pastry and cover with half of the custard mixture. Spread middle layer with marmalade and remaining custard mixture. Place on top. Spread top layer of pastry with reserved cream and decorate with slices of mandarin or orange.

Toast coconut under a hot grill until brown. Cool, then press a little onto top edge of pastry. Chill for up to 2 hours before serving.

To make in advance: Make the pastry layers and store in a tin for up to 5 days. Assemble just before serving.

AUTUMN LEAVES
Serves 6

Very simple to make using frozen pastry, and stunning to serve. Cut out a simple leaf shape template from card—or if you are clever, cut them out free style!

215-g/7½-oz packet frozen puff pastry, just thawed
a little beaten egg
500g/1lb fresh blackberries
225g/8oz cooking apples
1 teaspoon lemon juice
2 teaspoons sugar

Set oven at 230°C/450°F/Gas 8. Cut a leaf template from card. Roll out pastry to a 30-cm/12-in square. Cut out 6 pastry leaf shapes. Using the point of a knife, score another line about 5mm/¼in in from edge—in an oval shape—to make lid; lightly mark on veins of leaf. Brush with egg. Bake for 8–10 minutes or until risen and golden brown. Carefully loosen pastry lid using the tip of a knife and allow pastries to cool on a wire rack. Stew blackberries with 2 tablespoons water and 1 teaspoon sugar (or to taste) for five minutes. Allow to cool. Peel, core and slice apples. Stew with 3 tablespoons water, lemon juice and 1 teaspoon sugar.

To Serve: Place each pastry leaf on an individual plate. Reserve 6 tablespoons of blackberries. Divide the remaining between pastry cases with the apple slices. Press remaining blackberries through a sieve to purée. Serve with the pastries.

To make in advance: The pastry and the fruit can all be cooked 1 day in advance. Frozen fruit can also be used.

BASIC CHOUX PASTRY

Choux pastry makes lovely crisp containers for desserts. Use them freshly baked, or dry them out thoroughly in a warm oven and store in a cake tin for 1 week. Choux pastry can also be frozen; crisp it up in a hot oven for about 5 minutes before using.

CHOUX PASTRY

50g/2oz margarine
65g/2½oz plain flour
2 eggs

Place margarine in a small pan with 150ml/¼ pint cold water. Bring to the boil. Remove from the heat. Stir in all the flour at once. Beat with a wooden spoon until the mixture leaves the sides of the pan clean. If this does not happen after 1 minute, return to the heat and continue beating until it does. Cool slightly. Beat the eggs, add to the mixture a little at a time, beating well after each addition. Beat until the mixture is smooth and glossy. Use as for individual recipe.

MOCHA PROFITEROLES
Serves 8

The bitter coffee flavour helps balance the richness of the cream in this classic dessert. Use freshly made, ground coffee for the best flavour.

1 quantity choux pastry
300ml/½ pint double cream
icing sugar
4 tablespoons strong black coffee
100g/4oz plain dark chocolate

Set oven at 200°C/400°F/Gas 6. Grease two baking trays. Place choux pastry mixture in a nylon piping bag fitted with a 1-cm/½-in plain tube. Pipe 4 cm/1½ in rounds onto baking trays. Bake in oven for 25 minutes until firm and brown. Remove tray, slit the base of each with the point of a knife (to allow steam to escape) and allow to cool on a wire rack. Lightly whip the cream until it just holds its shape; place in a nylon piping bag fitted with a 1-cm/½-in plain tube. Pipe the cream through the slit in the base of each choux bun. Dust buns thickly with icing sugar. Chill. Place remaining cream in a greaseproof paper piping bag and snip end. Place coffee and chocolate together in a small pan. Stir until smooth. Pour sauce onto individual plates. Place profiterole in centre. Pipe cream around edge of plate and drizzle cream and chocolate over top.

STRAWBERRY CHOUX WITH COINTREAU CREAM

Magical mouthfuls—ideal for a buffet party. Make pastry in advance, and fill only a couple of hours before serving.

1 quantity choux pastry
300ml/½ pint double cream
2 tablespoons Cointreau or orange-flavoured liqueur
225g/8oz strawberries
icing sugar

Set oven at 200°C/400°F/Gas 6. Grease two baking sheets. Place choux pastry mixture in a nylon piping bag fitted with a 2.5-cm/1-in plain tube. Pipe 2.5 cm/1 in rounds on baking trays. Bake in oven for 10–15 minutes until firm and brown. Cut bottoms off of each bun. Cool.

Whip cream until it just holds its shape. Fold in Cointreau or liqueur. Sweeten with a little icing sugar if desired. Hull strawberries. Place a little cream in each bun. Push in a strawberry and spread base with a little more cream. Assemble and arrange on a serving plate. Dust with a little icing sugar.

BAKLAVA
Serves 12

This uses filo (or phyllo) pastry (sometimes called streudal leaves) that can generally be bought frozen from delicatessens and Continental food stores. This delicious dessert has layers of pastry and nuts soaked in a lemony syrup. It makes a lot, but will keep for up to 5 days.

225g/8oz sugar
3 tablespoons lemon juice
450-g/1-lb packet filo pastry
225g/8oz butter, melted
225g/8oz finely chopped mixed nuts—preferably walnuts

Set oven at 180°C/350°F/Gas 4. Place the sugar and lemon juice in a pan with 300ml/½ pint water. Dissolve over a low heat. Bring to the boil then simmer for 10 minutes. Cool. Grease a 30-cm/12-in roasting tin with melted butter. Lay 2 sheets of pastry in tin. Brush with melted butter. Layer another 2 sheets and repeat buttering and layering until you have 8 sheets. Cover with half of the nuts. Layer pastry and butter to give another 8 sheets, top with nuts and another layer of pastry. Brush the top of the pastry well with butter. Cut through the layers to mark the pastry into squares and then divide in half to make triangles. Bake for 30 minutes then reduce oven to 150°C/300°F/Gas 2 and cook for a further 1 hour until golden. Remove from the oven; allow to cool for 15 minutes, then pour over the syrup. Allow to cool completely.

CREAMY CAKES

BASIC WHISKED SPONGE

A light fluffy cake ideal for gâteaux and desserts filled with fresh cream or crème patissière and fruits. Flavour the cake to match the filling.

INGREDIENTS
2 eggs
50g/2oz caster sugar
50g/2oz plain flour

CAKE SIZE	COOKING TEMPERATURE	COOKING TIME
2 18cm/7in sandwich tins	180C°/350°F/Gas 4	15-20 minutes
1 20cm/8in sandwich tin	180C°/350F°/Gas 4	20-25 minutes
1 28 × 18cm/11 × 7in Swiss roll tin	200C°/400°F/Gas 6	5-8 minutes

Set oven (see chart). Grease and line the base of the cake tin; dust tin lightly with flour. Put the eggs and sugar in a bowl and cream until the mixture becomes thick and frothy like a mousse. The mixture should be thick enough to leave a definite trail when lifted. It is easiest to use an electric mixer, but if using a hand whisk, put the bowl over a saucepan of hot water. (The bowl must not touch the water or the eggs will cook.) Sift the flour and baking powder together. Carefully fold into the egg mixture using a large metal spoon. Be careful not to knock out all the air and cut through the mixture until all the flour is incorporated. Pour into a prepared tin. Shake the tin gently to level the mixture. Bake in the centre of the oven (see chart). Remove from the tin and leave to cool on a wire rack.

Flavourings

Chocolate: replace 25g/1oz flour with 25g/1oz cocoa
Coffee: and 1–2 teaspoons instant coffee to the egg-and-sugar-stage mixture
Orange/Lemon: add 1–2 teaspoons grated rind.

CRÈME PATISSIÈRE

This creamy custard is quite thick and firm and so will not run away or ooze out of delicate pastries!

300ml/½ pint milk
2 eggs
50g/2oz caster sugar
25g/1oz plain flour
½ teaspoon vanilla flavouring OR 1 vanilla pod
25g/1oz butter

Measure 2 tablespoons milk into basin. Stir in eggs, sugar and flour. Beat well until smooth. Boil remaining milk (with vanilla pod if used). Beat into egg mixture and return to pan. Cook, stirring, for 2 minutes or until thickened. Beat in vanilla flavouring and butter. Cover with cling film to prevent a skin forming.

ORANGE CRÈME GÂTEAU

Serves 8

Crumbly, creamy and not too sweet; make this cake and Crème patissière the day before if desired. Assemble the gâteau and leave for at least 2 hours before serving.

**2 orange-flavoured Whisked sponge cakes
    baked in two 20–cm/8–in round sandwich
    tins (recipe p.58)**
2 large thin skinned oranges
75g/3oz caster sugar
2 tablespoons Grand Marnier
1 quantity Crème patissière

Bake the cakes and leave on a wire rack until cool. Rinse cake tin and re-line the base with greaseproof paper. Thinly slice 1 orange, cover with cold water in a small pan, bring to the boil and simmer for 8–10 minutes until tender. Remove with a draining spoon and arrange in tin. Measure 150ml/¼ pint cooking liquid and return to the pan with sugar. Dissolve over a low heat then boil for 4 minutes or until syrupy. Spoon a little over the orange slices, reserve remainder. Place one round of cake on orange slices; sprinkle with orange syrup and Grand Marnier. Grate peel from remaining orange. Then cut of peel and white pith and segment fruit. Chop fruit and stir into the crème patissière with the orange rind. Spread over the cake and top with remaining round of cake. Sprinkle with remaining orange syrup and Grand Marnier. Chill until firm. Invert onto a serving plate, and served sliced.

BLACK FOREST GÂTEAU
Serves 14

Simply the best Black Forest I know, and worth all the effort.

CAKE
6 eggs, separated
125g/5oz caster sugar
50g/2oz plain flour, sifted
75g/3oz cornflour, sifted
56g/2oz cocoa, sifted

FILLING AND TOPPING
425-g/15-oz can pitted black cherries
2 teaspoons arrowroot
8 tablespoons Kirsch
450ml/¾ pint double cream
chocolate 'flock' or grated chocolate

Set oven at 180°C/350°F/Gas 4. Grease and line a 23-cm/9-in loose-bottom cake tin. Beat egg yolks with 6 tablespoons hand-hot water and caster sugar until thick and mousse-like. Whisk egg whites and a pinch of salt until stiff but not dry. Using a metal spoon, fold into mixture. Fold in flour, cornflour and cocoa. Pour into cake tin, bake for 1 hour. Turn out and cool. Drain cherries, reserving syrup. Set aside 14 cherries. Chop remainder and place in a pan with 6 tablespoons syrup. Blend in arrowroot. Bring to boil, stirring. Remove from heat and stir in 4 tablespoons Kirsch. Cut sponge in half. Sprinkle with Kirsch and sandwich with cherry mixture. Whip cream lightly. Spread top and sides of cake thinly with cream. Place remainder in a piping bag with a small star tube. Decorate with swirls of cream and cherries. Press chocolate around sides of cake.

To make in advance: The cake can be frozen (unfilled) for up to 2–3 months, or the decorated gâteau can be frozen for 1 month. Defrost in the fridge overnight.

ALMOND AND COFFEE CREAM CAKE
Serves 8–10

More of a dessert than a cake, and one that can be prepared at least one day in advance. Serve with single cream if liked.

CAKE

Whisked sponge cake (see p.58) baked in a 28 × 18cm/ 11 × 7in swiss roll tin.

FILLING

2 egg whites
100g/4oz icing sugar
225g/8oz unsalted butter, softened
1 tablespoon instant coffee powder
4 tablespoons apricot jam

TO DECORATE
100g/4oz flaked almonds, toasted
25g/10oz chocolate coffee beans

Make the cake and allow to cool on a wire rack.
To make the butter icing: whisk the egg whites and icing sugar together over a pan of hot but not boiling water until the mixture forms soft peaks. Beat the butter until soft, then gradually beat into the meringue mixture. Dissolve the coffee powder in 2 teaspoons hot water and beat into the icing. The mixture should be soft and satiny.

Cut the cake into three 7 × 18cm/3½ × 7in strips. Sandwich together with the apricot jam and just a little butter cream. Place on a serving plate. Place a quarter of the butter cream in a nylon piping bag fitted with a small star tube and spread remainder over top and sides of cake. Press toasted almonds against sides of cake; pipe top with butter cream; and decorate with chocolate coffee beans.

To Make in advance:
Store in fridge for up to 2 days or cover and freeze for up to 2 months. Defrost for 6 hours in a cool place.

EXCITING EXTRAS

CHOCOLATE SHAPES

Spread melted chocolate onto greaseproof paper or nonstick baking parcement and allow to set. Using pastry cutters, cut out shapes before chocolate is completely cold, or it will shatter.

CHOCOLATE TRELLIS CUPS

Place a large bun tray upside down and cover six alternate bun shapes with a little smooth cling film. Melt 100g/4oz plain dark chocolate. Place in a greaseproof paper piping bag and snip end. Pipe parallel lines in one direction over each bun tin. Then pipe in the opposite direction to form a trellis. Pipe around edge of bun tin in a circle to join up lines. Repeat to give a double trellis. Chill until set. Carefully lift off bun tin and peel away cling film. Keep chilled until ready to serve.

CHOCOLATE CARAQUE

Takes practice—but worth it!

Grate 75g/3oz plain chocolate, a small knob of butter and 2 teaspoons water, melt over a pan of hot water. Spread this thinly on a laminated surface. (Marble is better if you have it.) Leave until nearly set. It should not be too firm or it will not roll. Using a long, sharp knife shave it slant-wise, using a slight sawing movement and holding the knife almost upright. The chocolate should curl into long scrolls. Keep in a cool place until ready for use.

BRANDY SNAPS

An ideal accompaniment to ice creams and desserts, follow this recipe to make, curls, cups or small biscuits. They will store in a tin for up to 3 weeks.

3 level tablespoons golden syrup
50g/2oz margarine
50g/2oz caster sugar
1 teaspoon lemon juice
50g/2oz plain flour
1 teaspoon ground ginger

Set oven at 180°C/350°F/Gas 4. Line two baking sheets with non-stick baking parchment. Place syrup, margarine, sugar and lemon juice into a medium-sized pan. Heat gently until margarine has melted. Remove pan from heat, beat in flour and ginger. Place 2 tablespoons of mixture onto baking